Prayers for Your Journey

Inspired Words to Reflect & Remember

Sonia Jackson

Cover design by: Sonia Jackson

Printed in the United States of America

ISBN: 978-0-9619056-4-4

DEDICATION

To everyone who knows the power of prayer—and isn't afraid to use it.

To my parents, my family, my friends, and the ancestors who prayed me through things I didn't even know I'd need help with.

To the ministers, mentors, and sweet souls who guided me since I was little—even when I wasn't listening.

And to the Divine, who somehow manages to answer every time. Sometimes with a yes, sometimes with a "not yet," and sometimes with a loving side-eye.

Thank you. For the prayers, the presence, and the love.

CONTENTS

ACKNOWLEDGMENTS

Thank you…

Prayers for Your Journey began as a quiet nudge from Spirit and blossomed into these pages through the grace, love, and support of many souls. I honor my parents, who first placed prayer on my lips, and the Agape International Spiritual Center, where my practice deepened and found its wings.

To every person who has ever prayed for me—and to each heart I've held in prayer—know that your faith fuels mine. Special gratitude to my steadfast prayer companions and encouragers: Rev. Jean Hagan, Sonjia Burton, Lynndi Scott, Kathleen Spellman, Susanna Woods, Holly Alsop, Cynthia Chambers, Alicia Beavers, Chris Freeman, Laurel Harris, Maggie McCollester, Tammeron Karaim and Francesca James. Your wisdom, edits, gentle pushes, and fierce love carried this project across the finish line.

Finally, dear reader, thank you for choosing prayer as a tool for transformation. Each time you turn to these words, you not only bless your own path but ripple hope into our shared world.

Blessings on every step of your journey,

Sonia

WHAT IS PRAYER?

Simply put, prayer is a sacred conversation with a Higher Power. It is both deeply personal and universally understood. Whether whispered to the ocean, sung from a hymnal, spoken silently with a smile, or poured out through tears, prayer is how we align our spirit with Something Greater, with That which created the heavens and the Earth.

I grew up calling that Something Greater, "God," because that's what the people around me called It. Over time, I've come to know that It has many names: Yahweh, Lord, Jehovah, the Divine, Omnipresence, the Presence, and more. I use many of the names, but for my personal connection, my favorites are the Divine and Spirit.

The name we use doesn't matter as much as the energy with which we call the Presence. The energy of unconditional love, of pure reverence. The Most High listens to the heart of the one who is behind the saying of the name.

Prayer is how we remember who we are. It helps us align all that we are—mind, body, and soul—with the Omnipotent, Omnipresent, Omniscient Power that governs the universe. That's really all prayer is: alignment. To know, beyond a shadow of a doubt, that we are one with the Divine.

We are made in the image and likeness of God. That doesn't refer to our physical appearance. It means our spiritual essence. The energy of Spirit flows through all of creation, and because we are conscious beings, we carry that same energy within us. We have the ability to co-create with the Presence and shape the world we live in.

Notes:

_____

_____

_____

_____

_____

_____

_____

_____

_____

_____

_____

_____

_____

WHY PRAY?

There are as many reasons to pray as there are people.

Sometimes, we pray to say thank you, for life, for love, for the little things that make us smile. Sometimes, we pray for help, when life feels heavy, when we're uncertain, or when we or someone we love needs healing. Sometimes we pray simply to feel peace, or to be held by Something Bigger than ourselves.

Prayer is a powerful spiritual tool that allows us to express our deepest desires, seek guidance, offer gratitude, and find comfort and clarity.

Many years ago, I was introduced to Affirmative Prayer. It changed everything.

This kind of prayer isn't about begging, bargaining, or pleading. It's about knowing. It's rooted in faith, a deep trust that the good we seek already exists in the unseen and is waiting to be revealed. When we pray affirmatively, we speak from a place of realization. All is well. Right here. Right now. We know the prayer is already answered in Divine Mind, and we wait in expectancy, not in doubt.

But prayer is not just about getting something. It's about building a relationship with the Divine. It transforms us from the inside out. It aligns us with our higher wisdom. It softens us, strengthens us, and helps shape the desires of our hearts into alignment with our Highest Self.

Prayer changes things, but most importantly, prayer changes

us.

Notes:

_____

_____

_____

_____

_____

_____

_____

_____

_____

_____

_____

_____

_____

_____

_____

I PRAY

I believe all prayer works, but when we pray affirmatively, from the recognition of our oneness and union with Spirit, it places us in a more powerful stance. We're not speaking as someone in lack or need, but as someone who remembers who they are.

My first memory of prayer was when I was five years old and wanted to get my ears pierced. Around the same time, my parents were talking about buying a station wagon. Our old family car had no back seat, just two upside-down buckets where my brother and I would sit. It was time for an upgrade.

As children do, I overheard a conversation my parents had about me being too young for my ears to be pierced and the station wagon too much for my dad's teacher's salary. So, I prayed.

I pulled the little stool my father made for me in front of the mirror. I stood tall, looked myself in the eyes, and with all the conviction my little five-year-old self could muster, I began to declare: "I want a station wagon. I want my ears pierced. I want a station wagon. I want my ears pierced."

I repeated it like a mantra, like I knew it was going to happen. Until I felt it was going to happen.

And guess what? Within a short time, I got my ears pierced, and our family had a new station wagon. No more bucket seats.

That was my first prayer. My first answered prayer. My first manifestation, spoken like a bossy little five-year-old who knew the Universe was listening. And, It was!

Mother Teresa once said, "God speaks in the silence of the heart. Listening is the beginning of prayer." That's why, after the words have been spoken, we pause. We listen. We allow space for Spirit's response.

Reverend Michael Bernard Beckwith teaches that prayer is how we show Spirit we're open to receiving. Whether we kneel with heads bowed or stand with our faces lifted to the heavens, it's not the posture, it's the presence that matters.

Prayer is a sacred tool in my treasure chest of spiritual practices. It nourishes my connection with the Divine and keeps me in alignment with Spirit's purpose and the call of my Higher Self.

So, whether your prayers are spoken aloud or whispered in your heart, danced in joy or released through tears, know this: prayer is powerful. It is your lifeline. Your compass. Your sanctuary. Your sacred yes.

Notes:

_____

_____

_____

_____

_____

_____

_____

_____

_____

_____

_____

_____

_____

_____

_____

_____

_____

_____

_____

_____

_____

_____

_____

_____

_____

HOW TO USE THIS BOOK

These prayers were written through me, but they were written for you. They are your prayers now. You may not need every single one in this volume, but there may come a time when a prayer speaks directly to your situation or to someone you love.

Read it with them in mind. Say their name. Speak the words on their behalf.

One of my dear friends prefers short and sweet prayers. If that's you too, feel free to split a longer prayer into two. Or, if you've already felt the prayer, say "thank you" and "amen."

If a line doesn't resonate right now, skip it. Or, use a pencil to cross out what doesn't seem to work. Or, if it is a matter of believing that truth about yourself, re-read it until you do. This book is a living, breathing companion. Make it your own.

In my first book of prayers, My Prayer Journal, I suggested readers go through the prayers in order. That's not necessary here. Instead, when you're ready to begin, review the prayer titles and choose the one that speaks to your Spirit. Trust your intuition. It knows what you need.

Once you've selected a prayer, follow the guidance in the next section, Before You Begin, to prepare yourself. Give yourself a few sacred minutes, before and after prayer, to breathe, connect, and rest.

Notes:

_____

_____

_____

_____

_____

_____

_____

_____

_____

_____

_____

_____

_____

_____

_____

_____

BEFORE YOU BEGIN

Timing

The best time to pray? Whenever it comes to mind.

Prayer can be as simple as, "Thank you, God." But there's something sacred about greeting the day with a blessing before the world's noise begins; or, ending your evening with prayer just before you drift into sleep. Both are powerful times to align with peace.

Preparation

Get comfortable. Wear whatever makes you feel at ease. You don't have to change clothes, but if your waistband is too tight—loosen it. I suggest sitting rather than lying down so you stay alert and present.

Choose a location where you feel safe and relaxed: your living room, your garden, your favorite spot at the beach or park. Anywhere you can feel centered. Keep *Prayers for Your Journey* nearby and something to write with. If a message or idea comes to you, you'll want to catch it.

Breathing

When you're ready, allow yourself to move into a state of

relaxed awareness. Take a few deep, cleansing breaths. Inhale deeply, then exhale slowly. Breathe and relax. Do this a few times.

Sit in stillness and create a moment of gratitude you can truly feel in your body. Breathe and release. Then let your breath return to its natural rhythm.

Relax and Release

Settle into a comfortable position and gently scan your body from head to toe. Breathe into your neck and shoulders, unclench your jaw, release any tension. Relax your hands and fingers.

With each breath, let go of stress, worry, and concern. Allow yourself to soften into a peaceful, receptive state.

Keep your heart and mind open to what's possible. Trust that what you want is already moving toward you.

Gratitude

Now that you're more grounded and peaceful, bring your attention to something that brings a smile to your face. A moment, a memory, or a person that fills you with joy.

Let your heart rise in gratitude. Not just a thought of thanks, but a feeling. Something you can feel in your bones. From that sacred space, say "Thank you, Spirit," and then begin.

Selected Prayer

Read your selected prayer with your whole heart, silently or aloud. Close your eyes for a moment of reflection. Letting the words vibrate through your being. If thoughts, insights, or inspired ideas come to you, write them down.

Feel free to release what no longer fits and keep what lifts you higher. Know that it is your prayer.

If you come across a word you don't understand, I encourage you to look it up. Choose the meaning that speaks most clearly to your soul.

There are as many ways to use *Prayers for Your Journey* as there

are people on the planet. Find what works for you.
But this I know:
Spirit wants you to have the desires of your heart.
This is your journey. It's unique and always evolving. You ready?
Let's begin.

Notes:

_____

_____

_____

_____

_____

_____

_____

_____

_____

_____

_____

_____

_____

THE PRAYERS

I Am Creative

How grateful I am in this moment to pause and turn my awareness to the One Presence, the One Power, the Divine Source of all Creation. I rejoice in the infinite Intelligence that expresses through all of life, moving in, through, and as me.

This Presence is the Spirit of the Most High, the boundless Creative Force that formed the heavens and the Earth, the source of all inspiration, beauty, and wisdom. It is the Divine Spark that breathes life into all things, the eternal wellspring of creativity.

I am one with this Infinite Presence. The same Power that created galaxies, mountains, and oceans expresses as me. I am an individualization of Divine Intelligence, a vessel through which creativity flows. Spirit moves through my mind, heart, and hands, guiding me in all I create.

I stand confidently in the Truth that my gifts and talents are divine in origin. Spirit's ideas flow effortlessly through me, inspiring innovation, artistry, and new possibilities. Even in moments of doubt, I trust that I am divinely guided. I surrender to the creative impulse within, allowing my Light to shine brilliantly as an expression of the Most High.

I honor the sacred gifts Spirit has bestowed upon me, knowing that my creativity is a blessing to the world. I embrace my abilities with confidence and joy, allowing them to expand and unfold with grace. My work is meaningful, purposeful, and inspired, a reflection of Divine Intelligence at play.

I am profoundly grateful to witness the expression of Divine Truth and Love through my creativity. I celebrate the joy of inspiration, the beauty of divine ideas made manifest, and the boundless potential within me.

Knowing this prayer is already fulfilled, I release it into the Law of Love, trusting in its perfect unfoldment. With deep gratitude, I let it be. And so it is. Amen.

Affirmation: I transform my world through the expression of my loving gifts.

Notes:

_____

_____

_____

_____

_____

_____

_____

_____

_____

_____

_____

_____

_____

_____

_____

My Body Temple

With a deep and grateful breath, I acknowledge the breath of life as a sacred gift from God. I open my heart in gratitude for the divine intelligence that animates my being.

God, the Presence of the Most High, known by many names: Spirit, Eternal Love, the Universe, is the Source of all creation. There is no place where this Power is not, for it is the very essence of all that exists.

I recognize that Spirit birthed my soul out of Itself into this physical form. I am an extension of this Source Energy, a living expression of harmony, peace, power, and serenity. The same divine intelligence that moves the stars and the tides flows through my being. I am one with this Presence, and it moves through me in perfect alignment.

Honoring this truth, I bless my body temple as the sacred home of my Soul. I accept my body with love, appreciating its strength, resilience, and ability to heal. I affirm its vitality, its clarity, and its divine perfection in this moment. My voice is clear and kind, my senses are keen, and my mind is sharp. I celebrate my body's ability to move, to dance, and to express joy!

I release all that no longer serves me: beliefs, concerns, or limitations that are not in divine alignment with my highest good. I stand in self-acceptance, releasing judgment, guilt, or overindulgence. I call forth balance in my physical well-being, knowing it supports my mental and spiritual well-being. I honor myself with compassion, embracing the love of my Higher Self that is always present within me.

With deep gratitude, I affirm that this truth unfolds perfectly. I rejoice in my body's divine intelligence, knowing that all is well. I release this word into the infinite law of Spirit, knowing it is already fulfilled. And so it is. Amen.

Affirmation: I love my body as the temple that houses my Divine Spirit.

Notes:

_____

_____

_____

_____

_____

_____

_____

_____

_____

_____

_____

_____

_____

_____

_____

_____

_____

I Am Worthy

With a heart overflowing with gratitude, I acknowledge the Infinite Power of God, present everywhere, in everything, and in everyone. The Divine essence that created the heavens and the earth moves through me, expressing as my life.

I recognize that I am one with this Infinite Power. The same Divine Intelligence that orchestrates the universe flows through me, in me, and as me. I allow this truth to permeate my consciousness, dissolving all illusions of separation. I am an expression of the Divine, whole, complete, and worthy.

I open myself fully to Spirit, trusting that every need is met with divine precision. I release all thoughts of unworthiness, guilt, and shame. Peace fills my mind as I surrender to the truth of my divine nature. I let go of sadness, frustration, and helplessness, embracing the peace that is always available to me. I relinquish all fears of failure, knowing that I am supported, uplifted, and divinely guided.

I declare that my worth is inherent, not determined by external circumstances. Any doubts I once held about my value, my abilities, or my purpose are released now. Comparisons fall away as I stand firm in my authentic Self. Spirit transforms my insecurities into unwavering confidence, transmuting any feelings of inadequacy into self-acceptance and love.

I awaken to the truth that my Divine Higher Self is already present within me. The greatness I seek is not outside of me—it is who I am. Spirit guides me to embrace my uniqueness, to be comfortable and confident in my own skin. My value radiates from within, unshaken by external conditions.

The Presence moves through me, inspiring me to recognize my own magnificence. I am capable, focused, and worthy of success. As a child of the Most High, I am a one-of-a-kind emanation of Spirit, creative and joyful, fully aligned with the Divine's highest vision for my life.

I am deeply grateful to know that Spirit supports me in all ways, at all times. I give thanks for the love, wisdom, and confidence that are already mine. I rejoice in the unfolding of my highest potential, knowing that all is well.

With absolute trust in this truth, I release this word into the Infinite Law, knowing it is already fulfilled. I let it be, and it is so. Amen.

Affirmation: Today, I remember I am Spirit expressing powerfully. I am worthy because I Am.

Notes:

_____

_____

_____

_____

_____

_____

_____

_____

_____

_____

_____

_____

_____

My Potential

I pause to honor the sacred truth that I am evolving. I am grateful for the countless ways life has revealed the seeds of my greatness, even in moments I didn't fully see them. Each challenge, each breakthrough, each quiet whisper of intuition has led me to this knowing: my potential is divine in origin.

There is one Source, one Creative Intelligence that animates the stars and whispers possibilities into every soul. This Infinite Presence is Power, Purpose, and Pure Potentiality.

This same Presence lives within me. I am an emanation of Divine Intelligence, uniquely expressing the Infinite. I am not here by accident. I am here on purpose, with purpose. The greatness of God flows through me as ideas, energy, talents, visions, and dreams.

I now recognize and accept the fullness of my potential. I release any outdated beliefs or limiting stories that attempt to minimize the truth of who I am. I say yes to the call within me, to stretch, to rise, to shine. I am divinely equipped with everything I need to grow into the highest version of myself.

I give thanks for the infinite well of possibility that is always available. I give thanks for the courage to rise into my calling, for the support that meets me on the path, and for the joy that follows each aligned step I take.

With assurance, I place this prayer into the sacred rhythm of the Universe. Knowing it is so, I let it be. Amen.

Affirmation: I rise into the highest expression of myself. My potential is God in motion.

Notes:

_____

_____

_____

_____

_____

_____

_____

_____

_____

_____

_____

_____

_____

_____

_____

_____

_____

_____

_____

_____

_____

_____

_____

Embracing Change

I am in gratitude for the inner stability that Spirit provides, even when the world around me shifts. Awake and aware, I know I am always supported, no matter what transitions unfold. Change is not something I fear, it is something I know opens the door to growth.

The Source Energy is forever active and is unchanging in Its changelessness, and yet the source of all transformation. This Infinite Intelligence governs the tiniest cells and the galaxies, moving all things toward greater expressions of life. As an extension of this Energy, I allow myself to be led and shaped by the wisdom of God within.

Though external changes may seem uncertain, I trust the steady pulse of Spirit that guides me. I let go of old patterns and open my heart to new possibilities. Spirit flows through all circumstances, and even in discomfort, something higher is being revealed. I align myself with Divine Order and say yes to the unfolding good.

I look at all changes, allowing Spirit's peace that surpasses all human understanding to fill me, and I open to a greater realization of their significance. I am growing through whatever pain or heartache that may be present in the changes taking place.

Spirit moves through my life as clarity, courage, and peace that lift me during transitions. I give thanks for the divine solutions, supportive connections, and the perfect unfolding of every next step. Resources, supplies, funds, and assistance of every kind are revealed for the lives of all involved.

With a grounded heart and open mind, I release this word into the ever-responsive Law. The God Presence reveals Its Truth in my life with ease and effortlessness, so I know it is done. And so it is. Amen.

Affirmation: I move with grace through life's changes, guided by Spirit and grounded in peace.

Notes:

_____

_____

_____

_____

_____

_____

_____

_____

_____

_____

_____

_____

_____

_____

_____

I Heal

With deep gratitude, I open my heart to the Divine Presence that surrounds me. God is here, everywhere, in everything, and flowing through all of existence.

I turn inward, closing my eyes to the outer world, and feel the Presence within me. This sacred energy fills my heart, my being, and my entire existence. I am in the All, and the All is in me.

The Infinite expresses through me as perfect peace, boundless love, radiant health, and absolute well-being. Spirit moves through every function of my body, restoring, renewing, and revitalizing me at the deepest level. My body is a sacred temple, imbued with the intelligence of the Divine.

Every cell, every organ, every system within me operates in perfect harmony with Spirit. Any toxins, blockages, or imbalances dissolve in the Light of the Most High. I am cleansed, whole, and vibrantly alive. My energy is replenished, my strength restored, my vitality renewed.

I stand fully in the presence of pure Spirit, knowing that divine love is the healing force within me. I release all that no longer serves my highest good and allow the fullness of well-being to emerge.

With profound gratitude, I rest in the truth of my wholeness. I surrender to the divine unfolding, knowing that healing is already complete. I allow it to be revealed, and so it is. Amen.

Affirmation: Guided by the divine, my body revives and thrives.

Notes:

_____

_____

_____

_____

My Divine Healing

Rooted in deep appreciation, I embrace the blessings in all things: sunshine or rainfall, mountains or valleys, moments of ease or times of challenge. I give thanks for the divine guidance that moves through me each day, leading me with wisdom, strength, and clarity.

I recognize that Spirit, the Most High, is present everywhere, in all things, and as me. This Infinite Presence expresses through me as resilience, love, peace, and wholeness. The Divine moves through every aspect of my being, orchestrating perfect harmony in my body temple.

I affirm that this same Divine Presence moves through all those who support my healing—doctors, nurses, medical professionals, family, and friends. Each one is divinely guided, attuned to the highest wisdom, and blessed with clarity, compassion, and discernment. Every treatment, every word, and every action aligns with Divine Right Order, supporting my complete healing and well-being.

I bless any medicine, procedures, and nourishment I receive, knowing they serve as instruments of divine healing. Every cell in my body is infused with the light of wholeness. My body temple responds in perfect alignment, releasing all that no longer serves me and restoring itself with grace and ease. The intelligence of Spirit within me directs my healing, guiding me toward the right actions, the right care, and the right choices for my highest good.

I stand in this truth with unwavering faith, grateful for the divine perfection unfolding within me. Health, peace, and well-being are my birthright, and I claim them now. I rejoice in the awareness of my wholeness, knowing that healing is already happening.

I release this prayer into the loving hands of the Divine, trusting fully in its perfect fulfillment. With thanksgiving and joy, I let it be. And so it is. Amen.

Affirmation: I am in the flow of God's grace and the stream takes me to countless blessings.

Notes:

_____

_____

_____

_____

_____

_____

_____

_____

_____

_____

_____

_____

_____

_____

_____

_____

_____

Abundance & Plenty

With a heart full of gratitude, I accept this prayer as already fulfilled. I am thankful for the Presence of Spirit, which consistently meets every need and desire with love, grace, and perfect timing. I rejoice in the lavish generosity of the Universe.

There is One Power, One Source, One Divine Presence: Omniscient, Omnipresent, and unlimited. This Infinite Spirit is the governing intelligence behind all creation, and Its nature is abundance. Spirit expresses as endless good, boundless opportunities, radiant health, and overflowing love.

I am one with this Source. I am not separate from God. I am an individualized expression of the abundant nature of Spirit. All that God is, I am. This flow of divine plenty moves through me, in me, and as me.

Right here and now, I align with this truth. I recognize that all forms of wealth, money, ideas, friendships, health, time, love, are flowing freely into my life. I open myself fully to receive, to give, and to circulate these blessings with wisdom and joy. I am a faithful steward of this good.

Any illusion of lack or limitation is dissolved now. Old beliefs that no longer serve me are released into the nothingness from which they came. I stand fully in the truth of divine supply.

Gratefully, I celebrate the abundance that is already present and expanding. I am so thankful for the awareness of my oneness with Infinite Riches. I give thanks for the deepening of my consciousness and the prosperous life that is unfolding with ease.

And so, I joyfully release this prayer, knowing it is already done in the Mind of God. I let it be. And so it is. Amen.

Affirmation: I align all that I am with Spirit's Infinite Abundance.

Notes:

_____

_____

My Family's Health & Wholeness

I am truly grateful for the knowingness that there is only one Life. It is the Life of God, the Life of the Divine Presence that governs this Universe. This sacred Presence moves through the air we breathe, the trees, the flowers, Mother Earth, the Sun. All of nature sings with the Wholeness and Well-beingness of Spirit.

This Infinite Intelligence, beyond our thoughts and imaginings, reaches everywhere in the Universe and flows back to the very center of who and what I am. It is the essence of Love, Serenity, Harmony, and Wisdom, moving through all life and manifesting perfectly in all creation.

I know that the Power and Presence that is God is the very essence of me and each of my loved ones. This Divine Power is at the core of every member of my family. We are one with this Presence, unified in Its Infinite Love and Wholeness.

From this awareness, I call forth a healing for my family. I affirm a quickening of the Divine Life within every cell, organ, and activity of their body temples. Each cell is imbued with the power of God's love and vibrates at the highest level of healing. Anything unlike Health, Peace, or Wholeness is shaken off and dissolved.

I see love vibrating powerfully within each member of my family, restoring perfect balance, vitality, and peace in their minds, bodies, and spirits. Every glass of water they drink cleanses, renews, and flushes away toxins and impurities. Only Divine Well-being, Health, and Balance remain.

I affirm that Divine Wholeness is their Truth. I know that this rejuvenation and restoration is already happening with ease and grace.

How good it is to know that this Truth is already fulfilled! I am so grateful for the Divine Intelligence orchestrating this perfect healing and renewal in my family. I give thanks for the love, peace, and harmony now expressing fully in their lives.

With deep gratitude, I release this prayer into the Loving Law of the Divine, trusting it is already done in the mind of God. I trust completely in its perfect manifestation. I let it be, knowing the fullness and wholeness of life reveals itself effortlessly.

Thank You, Spirit. It is done. Amen.

Affirmation: My family feels the Loving Presence and vibrates with the wellness of Spirit.

Notes:

_____

_____

_____

_____

_____

_____

_____

_____

_____

_____

_____

_____

_____

_____

Open to Miracles

As I breathe and relax, I am deeply grateful for the Power Source that designed and created the heavens, the Earth, the Universe, and all that lies within. I give thanks for the awareness that this Power is present in my life and in all life, expressing infinite love and creativity.

This Power Source is Spirit. Dynamic, inventive, vibrant, and All-Knowing. It courses through my being, alive in every aspect of me. Spirit is soft yet powerful, abundant, and wise, providing all that is needed for a life of joy, peace, and fulfillment.

One with this Divine Power, I consciously tap into this eternal Source, which knows more about me than I could ever imagine. It lives in me and expresses through me. Spirit's guidance flows effortlessly within me, always leading me toward the highest good.

I open myself fully to Spirit's guidance, allowing miracles to reveal themselves in my life. I know a miracle is an act of God, and miracles are a natural expression of my alignment with Spirit. I trust in the abundance, wisdom, and joy of this Divine Source, knowing It provides for me in ways seen and unseen.

I declare prosperity, health, and wholeness in my life. The talents, skills, and abilities within me are magnified and expanded. Opportunities that are perfect for me come easily and naturally. Burdens are lifted, doubt and anxiety are released. I am joyfully energized.

Each day, I look for and recognize miracles. From the simple, such as unexpected blessings, to the complex, such as the orchestration of people, resources, and events for the fulfillment of my dreams. God's good continuously unfolds for me, multiplying exponentially in ways that amaze and delight me.

I am profoundly grateful for the abundance of miracles in my life. I give thanks for Spirit's infinite creativity and its continual expression through me. I celebrate the blessings I receive each day.

Knowing this prayer is already fulfilled in the mind of Infinite Intelligence, I release it into the Law of Love. I rest in this Truth and allow it to be.

Thank you, Spirit. And so it is done. Amen.

Affirmation: Open to the miracles in my life, I receive unlimited prosperity in all areas of my life.

Notes:

_____

_____

_____

_____

_____

_____

_____

_____

_____

_____

_____

_____

_____

_____

_____

_____

I Listen to Spirit

With an open heart and a deep vibration of gratitude, I acknowledge that God is all there is. The Divine presence moves through everything: the sun, the moon, the trees, the rocks, the air, the animals, and within me. I rejoice in the knowing that I am immersed in this Infinite Presence, always supported, always guided.

I recognize that the Lifeforce that sustains the universe is the same Lifeforce that breathes through me. I am made in the image and likeness of Spirit, infused with divine wisdom, clarity, and love. Spirit speaks to me always, and I set the intention to listen with clarity and discernment.

I am one with the Infinite Intelligence of the Universe. My spiritual nature guides my human experience, integrating both seamlessly. As co-creator with the Divine, everything in my life unfolds in divine order and absolute perfection. There is no separation between me and the wisdom of Spirit. I am connected, receptive, and attuned.

I declare that I am constantly guided by the still, small voice within. The voice of my Higher Self. I listen knowing Spirit directs my thoughts, words, and actions with insight and wisdom. Every day, before taking action, I tune in to the Divine, allowing it to lead my steps in my meetings, projects, and personal moments. Doubts and concerns dissolve as I surrender to this sacred wisdom.

I open fully to the messages of Spirit, sensing pathways being cleared before me. I receive answers in the form of peaceful, easy messages—an inner knowing, a gentle nudge, a feeling of certainty, an inspiration to call someone or visit a place. The foundation of my life is Divine Spirit, and from this sacred alignment, my creativity flows freely, my actions are purposeful, and my path is illuminated.

How good it is to trust this truth! I am deeply grateful that Spirit speaks to me in ways I understand. Grateful that my life is unfolding in perfect harmony. Grateful that every moment is an opportunity to listen, trust, and act in alignment with the Divine.

With joy and faith, I release this prayer into the loving hands of the Most High, knowing it is already done. I rest in this truth and I let it to be. So it is done. Amen.

Affirmation: I listen with trust, wisdom, and unwavering faith, knowing the voice of Spirit always speaks clearly within me.

Notes:

_____

_____

_____

_____

_____

_____

_____

_____

_____

_____

_____

_____

_____

_____

_____

Clarity & Discernment

I begin with deep appreciation for the gift of consciousness. The sacred ability to reflect, to choose and to grow. I am grateful for the countless ways clarity has already shown up in my life, sometimes subtle, sometimes bold, but always present when I pause and listen.

There is only One Presence, One Power, One Infinite Intelligence that knows all, sees all, and is All. This Presence is the Source of wisdom and discernment. It is the all-knowing activity of God expressing Itself through and as creation.

This Divine Presence and I are not separate. I am one with the Infinite Mind, one with the clarity and vision of Spirit. As I attune myself to this sacred inner compass, I trust the way will always be revealed. I move with the assurance that I am never without guidance.

I affirm that Divine Discernment is active in every area of my life. I see clearly what is mine to do. I listen deeply and make decisions from a place of spiritual alignment. My thoughts are ordered, my choices refined by wisdom. In my work, relationships, and personal growth, I am guided by the high vibration of Truth.

How thankful I am to stand in this awareness, to know that I don't need to chase answers. They live within me. I give thanks for every gentle nudge, every insight, every peaceful pause that makes the path ahead more evident.

I now release this word into the Universal Law, knowing the clarity I seek is already mine. The God Presence reveals Its Truth in my life with ease and effortlessness, so I know it is done and can let it be. Amen.

Affirmation: I am divinely guided in all things. I see with clarity. I choose with discernment.

Notes:

_____

_____

_____

_____

_____

_____

_____

_____

_____

_____

_____

_____

_____

_____

_____

_____

_____

_____

I am Financially Free!!

I begin in gratitude for the gift of the awareness of the abundant possibilities that surround me. Thank you, Spirit, for life and for the opportunity to thrive.

There is one Source, one Divine Presence that is limitless in its giving, Prosperity Itself. This Infinite Intelligence expresses as all of creation, and as me. I am a divine emanation of this Source, inseparable from its love, abundance, and infinite supply.

As I rest in this truth, I affirm my oneness with the principle of prosperity. Spirit's idea of wealth is boundless. Beyond material means, it is joy, freedom, well-being, and flow.

I accept financial freedom as my divine inheritance. I claim the ability to make life choices not from fear or limitation, but from passion, purpose, and peace.

I am divinely supported. All that I need,resources, income, wisdom, right relationships, s already prepared. I release any guilt, shame, or past missteps, knowing they are dissolved in the light of awareness. I am free to prosper. Free to live. Free to give.

New avenues of income, expansion, and creativity are unfolding. Spirit guides me to aligned opportunities that reflect the truth of who I am and what I have to offer the world.

I give generously from the overflow and bless others with kindness and grace.

With deep gratitude, I give thanks for this revelation of Truth, for the manifestation already set in motion. I allow it to be and it is. Amen.

Affirmation: I am open to unlimited abundance. Financial freedom is mine, and I live in joyful flow.

Notes:

_____

_____

_____

_____

_____

_____

_____

_____

_____

_____

_____

_____

_____

_____

_____

_____

_____

_____

Time is on My Side

How grateful I am to recognize the beauty of life, the ever-present divine support surrounding me. Like the sky that remains blue beyond any clouds, I trust that God's infinite abundance and wisdom are always present.

I acknowledge the Divine as the Source of all life, the eternal force that moves through time and space, unbound by human limitations. Spirit is Infinite, Omnipresent, and Omnipotent, always working for my highest and best. This Divine Intelligence governs all things, including my time, my finances, and my creative expression.

I am one with this Divine Intelligence that orchestrates the universe within me. In this sacred union, I align myself with the divine flow, knowing that my work, my finances, and my artistry, are seamlessly integrated into God's perfect plan for me. I no longer struggle with time, for time is on my side, working in harmony with my divine purpose.

I call forth clarity, balance, and ease as I align my daily actions with my greater vision. I release any sense of overwhelm and instead embrace divine order. My work supports me financially in perfect ways, allowing me to thrive while pursuing my passions. Resources, opportunities, and inspired ideas flow effortlessly to me.

I attract clients and experiences that align with my divine purpose, bringing joy and fulfillment. I walk confidently toward my future, knowing that God's plan exceeds my greatest imagination. I release stress and anxiety and claim my abundance now, knowing my every financial need is met. Every dream placed in my heart by Spirit is unfolding in perfect time.

I am deeply grateful for this truth. Grateful for divine timing, divine guidance, and divine provision. I rejoice in the knowing that my desires and aspirations are already being fulfilled. My heart overflows with appreciation as I witness Spirit's magnificent plan unfolding in my life.

With faith and trust, I release this prayer to Spirit, knowing that it is already done. I surrender to divine order and allow time to work in my favor. I let go and I let it be. Amen.

Affirmation: I am in the right place at the right time and take inspired action on the possibilities that unfold.

Notes:

_____

_____

_____

_____

_____

_____

_____

_____

_____

_____

_____

_____

_____

_____

_____

_____

My Act Two

How grateful I am to know that Spirit is the Source of all creation—the infinite intelligence, wisdom, and love that moves through all of existence. I rejoice in the knowing that this Divine Presence is ever-present, guiding and unfolding my life in perfect harmony.

Spirit is the very essence of all that is. It is the creative force behind every possibility, every new beginning, and every unfolding chapter. As the existence of all, I recognize that this boundless presence lives and breathes within me. I am one with the Infinite, and within this sacred unity, I stand in the fullness of Divine wisdom and grace.

From this deep place of Oneness, I affirm clarity for this next phase of my life. I embrace the shifts, the changes, and the stirrings in my soul that whisper, "There is more for me." I release resistance and allow Divine guidance to flow through me. I honor the knowing that my journey is evolving, and I trust that Spirit's plan for me is greater than I can imagine.

I welcome this new Act Two in my life and career. I surrender the old, making space for the fresh, the vibrant, and the inspired. Spirit speaks to me, and I listen. I step forward with faith, open to new talents, skills, and callings that emerge with ease and grace. I allow the Divine to mold me into an even more dynamic expression of love and purpose. I clearly see who I am here to serve, and I move forward with confidence.

A new legacy, once dormant, now awakens within me. Spirit aligns everything I need, connections, opportunities, and divine inspiration, whispering on a light breeze, striking like bolts of clarity. I am the conduit for this next expression of my life, and I allow it to take shape with divine ease.

I am grateful for this Truth, for the knowing that all is unfolding perfectly. I give thanks for my willingness to step into the fullness of this next chapter. I celebrate the divine orchestration of every detail, trusting that Spirit knows what to do, how to do it, and provides the perfect steps for me to follow.

With deep trust, I release this prayer into the hands of the Most High. Knowing it is already done, I allow it to unfold in divine timing and perfect order. And so it is. Amen.

Affirmation: My journey is paved with golden opportunities.

Notes:

_____

_____

_____

_____

_____

_____

_____

_____

_____

_____

_____

_____

_____

_____

_____

Allowing Me

Note: Greatness isn't reserved for celebrities, icons, or historic figures. Greatness lives in each of us. It's the courage to be authentic, to fully express the all of who we are in our daily lives. Your joy, your voice, your compassion, your creativity, these are all expressions of your unique greatness. This prayer is a reminder that allowing your full self to shine is a divine act.

With deep gratitude, I acknowledge the life moving through me. The sacred rhythm of my beating heart that reminds me I am here on purpose. I give thanks for the blessings that surround me and flow through me, evidence of Spirit's loving presence.

I recognize that there is only One Power, One Infinite Presence, God, the Divine, Spirit, expressing as all creation. This Presence is everywhere, in everything, and most powerfully, right here within me.

I am one with this Presence. Spirit individualized Itself as me. The greatness of God expresses uniquely through my being. I am a divine idea unfolding in perfect alignment with Infinite Intelligence.

In this awareness, I release the beliefs and projections of others about who I should be. I let go of old stories, doubts, and limitations. I open to the truth of who I am: whole, worthy, powerful, and free. I honor my voice, my gifts, my path. I allow my authenticity to rise and be seen. I embrace my growth and my becoming, revealing my wholeness and my personal perfection.

I now choose to love myself fully. My relationship with myself is sacred, rooted in truth and compassion. I allow Divine Love to guide every relationship in my life, beginning with the one I have with me. I stand in acceptance, in peace, in power.

With a grateful heart, I give thanks for the knowing, and the divine alignment now unfolding. I bless the journey that brought me to this moment, and I celebrate the greatness that I am.

I release this word into the Law, knowing it is already done in the Mind of God. And so it is. Amen.

Affirmation: My individuality makes me unique, and I stand out and shine!

Notes:

Healing Generational Trauma
A Prayer for Women*
*Option: This prayer was written with women in mind, however, if the content of the prayer applies to you, feel free to change the nouns so you can read it with ease. Make it for all ancestors, not just the feminine side.

I am deeply thankful for the Spirit of the Most High, the Divine Presence that is the essence of all creation, from the beauty of a garden to the joy in a child's laughter. I am filled with gratitude for Spirit, ever-present and ever-loving,

This Infinite Presence is the source of all life, the wellspring of love, wisdom, and power. It flows through all that is and expresses itself through me. I recognize that this Presence has shaped me into the loving, kind, understanding, and intelligent being that I am.

I know I am one with Spirit, inseparably connected to the Infinite. In this truth, I see every woman in my lineage as a powerful spiritual being, connected to this same Divine Source. Through the ages, they have tapped into this Infinite Presence, guided by love and wisdom, despite the challenges of their times.

I call forth a healing for my lineage. A healing across time, space, and all dimensions. I affirm that any destructive historical situations, traumas, or plights are now transformed by the power of the Divine Love. I see every ancestor as vibrant, strong, and resourceful. I bless and forgive any perceived missteps, knowing that they have brought us to this moment of blessing and opportunity.

I release societal limitations and false narratives about my ancestors. I see them as the powerful teachers, scientists, and creators they truly are, paving the way for future generations. I honor their resilience, wisdom, and endurance, which have given me and others the freedom to live with expanded possibilities.

As I stand in this lineage of strength, I release all concerns, thoughts, and ideas contrary to the truth of our Divine essence. I let go of generational trauma, abuse, and limiting beliefs, allowing healing to flow freely through me, through my family. I embrace the truth that I am the Divine in expression.

I am profoundly grateful for the grace, resilience, and

enduring spirit of the women in my ancestry. I give thanks for the hope, strength, and blessings they birthed into future generations, including me.

Knowing this prayer is already fulfilled in the mind of God, I release it fully, trusting in its perfect unfolding. I let it fly, knowing healing and wholeness are now revealed. And so it is. Amen.

Affirmation: I am the embodiment of Divine Healing—now, and for generations to come.

Notes:

_____

_____

_____

_____

_____

_____

_____

_____

_____

_____

_____

_____

Phoenix Rising

Grateful for the eternal presence of Spirit, I turn inward to the one true Power, Divine Love, that holds me through all seasons, all storms. This Love is deeper than loss, higher than despair, and stronger than any condition I face.

I recognize this Love as God, as Spirit, as the Infinite Intelligence that governs all. It is the Source of Life Itself. It moves through every breath, every heartbeat, every unfolding moment. This sacred Presence is not only around me—it expresses as me.

From this sacred awareness of Oneness, I speak this word for my life: I rise. I rise from every limitation, betrayal, hardship, and heartbreak. No longer defined by pain or circumstance, I release fear, doubt, and the ashes of my past. I call forth the Divine Power within me to reclaim my strength, my dignity, my wholeness.

I walk away from anything that does not honor the truth of who I am. I am renewed through Spirit's wisdom. I am transformed by Divine fire, not consumed by it, but reborn. I stand in full faith that I am guided, lifted, and supported in every way.

How grateful I am for this sacred rising, for the truth that I am never alone, and for the strength that now courses through me. I bless this becoming. I give thanks for new vision, for new wings, for new heights. I give thanks that I rise.

I release this word into the heart of Spirit, trusting its perfect unfolding.

The God Presence reveals Its Truth in my life with ease and effortlessness, so I know it is done. And so it is. Amen.

Affirmation: From the ashes, I rise. Stronger, wiser, and rooted in Divine Truth.

Notes:

Courage to Be

Embracing the fullness of grace, I acknowledge the strength and power of the Universe reflected in the majestic mountains, the towering redwoods, and the churning sea. I see and feel the wonder of this divine strength, and I allow it to fill me.

I recognize that the Source of all creation, the Omnipresent Power that forms and sustains everything, is within me. The same Love, Truth, Peace, and Wisdom that created the universe lives at the core of my being. I am one with this infinite Presence, and it expresses through me in all I do.

From this sacred connection, I call forth the courage to be my authentic self. I stand in my truth with boldness and clarity. I speak up and speak out. I embrace the possibilities that are unfolding for me.

Any wounds from past untruths are now healed. I no longer hide my light. I shine brightly in all my activities and in every situation.

I move through life with fearless grace, trusting Spirit's guidance in every step I take. I have the courage to love myself fully, to embrace who I am now and who I am becoming. I listen deeply to the wisdom within and follow my dreams with confidence. I say "no" without fear, knowing that it often means I am saying "yes" to my highest good.

I rest in the knowing that the strength and courage I seek have always been within me. Spirit has equipped me with all that I need. I accept this truth. I give thanks for the knowing I allow it to be. And so it is. Amen.

Affirmation: Guided by the Divine, I boldly step out In Life therefore I am unstoppable.

Notes:

_____

_____

_____

_____

_____

_____

_____

_____

_____

_____

_____

_____

_____

_____

_____

_____

_____

_____

_____

_____

My Divine Mate

Breathing in gratitude for the infinite love of Spirit that fills my heart, I relax. I am at peace, knowing I am held in the Divine embrace. With each breath, I am nurtured by the boundless love that surrounds and flows through me.

The Love and Light of Spirit, which governs the Universe, moves through my being, activating my heart at its deepest core. I am one with the All. One with love, joy, harmony, wisdom, and divine intelligence. This Presence within me is the very source of all relationships rooted in truth, wholeness, and sacred union.

Standing in this awareness, I allow the light of the Most High to shine through me, illuminating the path that leads me to my Divine Mate. We are already connected in Spirit, moving toward each other in perfect alignment. Guided by the wisdom of the Divine, I walk with an open heart, knowing that love is drawing us together effortlessly.

I affirm that when we meet, our connection is instant, harmonious, and filled with joy. We recognize the beauty within each other's hearts, and our souls resonate in divine love. I trust the process, knowing that all is unfolding in divine order. Every step I take is divinely orchestrated, leading me to the fulfillment of this sacred partnership.

Even now, I feel the quickening of our hearts. I surrender to the knowing that this love is already here, already alive within me. It is not something I must search for—it is something I allow. Spirit is guiding us toward one another, drawing us closer with the magnetic force of divine love.

How grateful I am to trust in the perfect unfolding of this love. I give thanks for the joy, the connection, and the deep companionship that is already mine. I celebrate the beauty of divine timing and the love that continues to reveal itself in my life. My heart overflows with appreciation.

With unwavering faith, I release this prayer into the loving hands of the Most High. I trust that it is already fulfilled in the mind of Spirit.

I let go, knowing that all is well, and I open myself fully to receiving the love that is destined for me. With joy and thanksgiving, I let it be. And so it is. Amen.

Affirmation: Keeping my heart open, I am joyously washed in Spirit's love and release it drawing more love to me.

Notes:

_____

_____

_____

_____

_____

_____

_____

_____

_____

_____

_____

_____

_____

_____

_____

_____

Fulfillment

How grateful I am for the knowingness and understanding that God is. I am filled with gratitude for the Presence of Spirit, which is always guiding, nurturing, and supporting me in every way.

God is the Presence, the Omnipotent, Omniscient Source of all creation, everywhere present. This Divine Intelligence beats my heart, breathes my breath, and moves through all aspects of my being. Spirit is the essence of joy, abundance, and infinite possibility, expressing Itself in and as all life.

I know that this Presence is the very core of who and what I am. I am one with this Infinite Source, inseparably connected to Its wisdom, love, and creativity. The Divine Presence flows through me, as me, and is me.

In union with Spirit, I am guided by Divine Wisdom and aligned with Infinite Opportunities. I open myself to the light within, and to the fulfillment of my heart's desires. Ideas flow to me effortlessly, inspired by the Spirit of the Most High.

I recognize there are dormant talents within me and know they are ready to emerge and expand. My Higher Self aligns me with purposeful, meaningful work that reflects my values and allows all that I am to shine.

The vibration of Divine Good floods my soul with enthusiasm, expectancy, and peace. I feel the joy Spirit has gifted me, and I trust in Its perfect timing as my path unfolds with ease and grace.

I am so grateful to know that all I need is already within me, and that Spirit is constantly revealing everything I require for my highest good. I trust in its perfect manifestation.

With deep gratitude and faith, I release this prayer into the infinite law of Mind, knowing it is already done in the mind of God. I accept the guidance, embrace the good, and allow it all to be. And so it is. Amen.

Affirmation: As I stand at the door of possibility and knock, opportunity answers.

Notes:

I Speak with Confidence

Opening myself in reverent gratitude, I center myself in the gift of my breath. As I feel the rise and fall of my chest, I know that all is well. I give thanks for this sacred moment, for the life force that flows through me, and for the Divine Presence that speaks in and through me.

God, the Infinite Creative Power, is everywhere in Its fullness. Spirit is Omniscient, Omnipotent, and ever-present. This Divine Intelligence moves through all things, and it moves through me. I am in perfect communion with the Most High, I trust this Presence within me.

Rooted in this truth, I give voice to my soul's desires. I call forth the confidence and power that Spirit has already placed within me. Peace and harmony are present in every word I speak, and divine wisdom guides my expression.

I speak with clarity, assuredness, and purpose. I know that the message I share is needed, and I trust that it reaches those who are meant to hear it. Whether I am speaking in a meeting, in a personal conversation, or before an audience, my words flow with grace and ease, aligned with the truth of Spirit.

Every word that passes my lips is a reflection of Divine Love, guided by wisdom and delivered with understanding. I speak, I sing, I write, and I express myself with the confidence of Spirit. Joyfully and powerfully, I allow the fullness of my voice to be heard through my heart.

I give thanks for this divine unfolding, knowing that this truth is already established. I release this prayer into the law of the Universe, trusting that it is fulfilled. And so it is. Amen.

Affirmation: I use my voice to speak my Truth powerfully.

Notes:

_____

_____

Prayers for Your Journey

_____

_____

_____

_____

_____

_____

_____

_____

_____

_____

_____

_____

_____

_____

_____

MORE PRAYERS

Great Spirit Prayer

Oh, Great Spirit,
Whose voice I hear in the wind
and whose breath gives life to all the world.
Hear me! I need your strength and wisdom.
Let me walk in beauty, and make my eyes
ever behold the red and purple sunset.
Make my hands respect the things you have made
and my ears sharp to hear your voice.
Make me wise so that I may understand
the things you have taught my people.

Help me remain calm and strong in the
face of all that comes towards me.
Let me learn the lessons you have hidden
in every leaf and rock.
Help me seek pure thoughts and act with
the intention of helping others.
Help me find compassion without
empathy overwhelming me.
I seek strength, not to be greater than my brother,
but to fight my greatest enemy: Myself.
Make me always ready to come to you

with clean hands and straight eyes.
So when life fades, as the fading sunset,
my spirit may come to you without shame.

- Translated by Lakota Sioux Chief Yellow Lark in 1887

Notes:

_____

_____

_____

_____

The Serenity Prayer

God, grant me the serenity to accept the things I cannot
change,
The courage to change the things I can, and
The wisdom to know the difference.

- Excerpted from Reinhold Niebuhr's Poem

Notes:

_____

_____

_____

_____

An Old Irish Blessing

May the road rise up to meet you.
May the wind be always at your back.
May the sun shine warm upon your face; the rains fall soft upon your fields.
And until we meet again, may God hold you in the palm of His hand.

-Traditional

Notes:

_____

_____

_____

_____

A Psalm of David
As revised by Sonia Jackson

The Lord is my shepherd, so I have everything I need.

Spirit has given me green pastures where I rest,
I am lead beside peaceful waters,
    and my soul is nourished.

I am guided along the right paths
    by the Divine.

Even though I walk
    through the darkest valley,
I will fear no evil,

for Spirit is with me;
It's rod and staff,
   comfort me.

Spirit prepares a feast before me
   in the presence of my enemies.

My head is anointed with oil;
   my cup overflows.

Spirit's goodness and love follows me
   all the days of my life,
and so I dwell in Spirit, in the house of the Lord
   forever.

Originally Psalm 23 from the Holy Bible.

Notes:

_____

_____

_____

_____

_____

_____

_____

_____

_____

MORE AFFIRMATIONS

My body vibrates with the wellness of the Divine.

My mind, body and spirit work in harmony to create a life that flourishes.

I am the very emanation of Source Energy, a radiant being sizzling with life force!

I immerse myself fully in Spirit's richness, becoming a vessel overflowing with divine love.

I accept I am worthy of the boundless goodness that flows from the Divine.

I move through Spirit's Garden of Infinite Possibilities and breathe in their vibrant essence, making them my own.

Opportunities that resonate deeply with my heart's desires now appear before me. Joyfully, I embrace each one.

I wholeheartedly embrace myself – my most authentic self, and I am undeniably Enough!

My life pulsates with the brilliant opportunities bestowed by the Most High.

My life springs forth from an inexhaustible wellspring of God's goodness, overflowing with abundance, pure joy, and unconditional love.

Guided by the Divine, I am magnetized to forces and resources that support my heart's desires.

Tapping into my Inner Wisdom, I effortlessly align with my life's purpose and projects.

My path is divinely lined with abundant blessings at every turn.

Fired up by the Presence within, my confidence glows and grows.

The inherent abundance and prosperity that already courses through me now expands exponentially.

My Inner Wisdom helps me reveal more clarity, courage and confidence, creating a limitless flow in my life.

Listening to the Most High, I take inspired action and my highest potential blossoms.

Pathways of possibility unfold with abundant ease and divine grace in my life.

Thank you, Spirit, for the unique talents, inherent gifts, and boundless creativity that reside within me.

The abundant blessings of the Most High pour into every aspect of my existence.

Today, I am open and receptive to the glorious surprises that

Spirit has in store for me!

God's life moves through me as healing energy, so I know every cell of my body vibrates with Love.

Notes:

APPENDIX

Affirmative Prayer Steps

Step One – Gratitude

"As you begin to be grateful for what most people take for granted, the vibration of gratitude makes you more receptive to good in your life."

– Reverend Michael Bernard Beckwith

We begin by cultivating a sense of gratitude and appreciation by focusing on the positive aspects of our desires. This allows us to shift from worries and doubts. Letting go of any troubling situations we may be facing and letting gratitude be the dominant thought, not only in your awareness, but to also feel the gratitude with our whole body, opens us to the good that surrounds us.

Find something to be grateful for, anything from waking up in the morning, to the beating of your heart, to the beauty of a flower, to the smile of a child, anything you can feel. Let gratitude and thoughts of appreciation vibrate within your cells of your being and see if you detect a visceral feeling.

Step Two - Recognition

In Step Two, we speak of our recognition of God as all there is. There is only God everywhere present, one Love, one Energy, one Force, the Source of all creation is Omnipotent, Omnipresent and Omniscient. Let this recognition and acknowledgement pervade your consciousness.

Step Three – Unification

It's a natural progression to move from Step Two Recognition to Step Three Unification because all there is, is the Divine. The Divine is everything. Everything was birth from Spirit. We are birthed from Spirit as unique and individualized emanations. Acknowledging our Oneness with the Divine and recognizing that we are all connected spiritually. We are Spiritual beings having a human experience.

Step Four – Realization

As in Step Three, we recognize the Divine Presence within. The Presence created the heavens and the Earth, and being made in Its image and likeness, not our physical face in the mirror, but our consciousness, we are able to create our world. Our consciousness awareness will determine what that world will look like.

We are one with all that exists. With Step Four, we move to the realization, we are one with our heart's desires.

In other words, recognizing God as Omnipresent, we realized we are inherently connected to all desires through the Divine Presence within.

Step Five – Thanksgiving

Thanksgiving is a return to gratitude and appreciation to open to our good. We stand in one of God's promises, that when we ask, it is given. (Matthew 7:7-8) with this Truth, we know our heart's desires as already fulfilled.

What we focus on, we manifest. So we focus on gratitude, joy, peace, harmony. We give thanks for all that we've received. We give thanks for all that's been realized.

Step Six - Release

We release the prayer, trusting Spirit has already answered. We release the prayer into the all-powerful, all knowingness of Divine Intelligence. Like a seed that has been planted in the soil, we let the Divine do the work. We allow ourselves to move through time and space, doing what we need to as we move forward, in joyful anticipation of the prayer's manifestation.

The prayer is like an unopened present for your birthday. Your friend always gets you what you asked for. As you await the big day, you are in celebration and accept that it is done. Amen.

Affirmation: Magic moments happen all around me. I see and receive them with joy!

Notes:

_____

_____

_____

_____

_____

_____

_____

_____

_____

_____

_____

ABOUT THE AUTHOR

Sonia Jackson is an accomplished playwright, director, and spiritual practitioner trained at the Agape International Spiritual Center in Los Angeles. With more than 25 years of service as an affirmative-prayer practitioner, and over 14,000 spoken prayers, she brings deep spiritual grounding, compassion, and creative insight to everything she does. Through her nonprofit Visions of Possibilities, Sonia dedicates herself to uplifting women and all who seek a stronger sense of worth, voice, and divine power. Her community-wide Healing Prayer Parties create welcoming spaces where people of every background unite in shared prayer and possibility. *Prayers for Your Journey* furthers her lifelong mission to open hearts, expand horizons, and remind us that, together, we can transform the world—one prayer at a time.